Follow and Do

Confession

Follow and Do

Confession

Written and Illustrated by Joni Walker

CONCORDIA PUBLISHING HOUSE · SAINT LOUIS

Published by Concordia Publishing House
3558 S. Jefferson Avenue, St. Louis, MO 63118-3968
1-800-325-3040 · cph.org

Manufactured in China/055760/418582.

9 10 11 12 13 14 15 16 17 18 35 34 33 32 31 30 29 28 27 26

For Diana,

We really did grow up to be artists.

Dear Parents,

Confession, and the Office of the Keys, is the "doing" behind what we pray in the Lord's Prayer: "forgive us our trespasses as we forgive those who trespass against us."

We are to CONFESS our sin against our neighbor. We are also to forgive our neighbor who sins against us. Parents model this with and for their children. Not only should children learn to say "I'm sorry" when they do something wrong, but parents should learn to respond with "you are forgiven." To respond with a simple, "it's okay," misses the freedom that forgiveness brings.

"Forgiven" means two things. First, you are no longer guilty, which means, second, the wronged person no longer has anything to hold against you. A child who is consistently forgiven is all the more aware of the gifts of his Baptism, the washing & renewal.

The second aspect comes in the Office of the Keys where we acknowledge (confess) that all our wrongs are sins, ultimately, against God. In this part of the catechism, we hear that when we confess our sins to the pastor, he will speak to us the truth that God sets aside His judgment against sin, for Jesus' sake. Through the authority given by God, our pastor can extend to us the forgiveness of God.

What comfort it is for guilty consciences to hear that what God's Son did 2,000 years ago is for you right now, today. Jesus Christ died for the sins of the world, even yours, even your child's. Admitting and confessing our SINS is a difficult thing. But as Christians, we can be confident that we are forgiven in Christ and that we can forgive others.

Luther said that parents are the priests of the family. When it becomes the family's practice to confess and forgive sins, children are strengthened and learn to value confession. Then, they value even more the forgiveness that is theirs as God's own children.

What is Confession?

Confession has two parts.
First, that we confess our sins.

I am sorry for
the bad things
I have done.

And second, that we receive absolution, that is, forgiveness, from the pastor as from God Himself, not doubting, but firmly believing that by it our sins are forgiven before God in heaven.

I believe God forgives me.

What sins should we confess?

Before God we should plead guilty
of all sins, even those we are not aware of,
as we do in the Lord's Prayer;

When I ask God
to forgive me, He
forgives all of
my sins.

I feel badly for
the way I acted today.

But before the pastor we should confess only those sins which we know and feel in our hearts.

Which are these?

Consider your place in life according to the Ten Commandments:

Are you a son, daughter, sister, brother or student?
Have you been disobedient or lazy?

Have you been hot-tempered, rude or quarrelsome?

DINOSAURS

Have you hurt someone by your words or deed?

I made fun of a girl in my class.

LITTLE TURTLE ELE

Have you stolen, been negligent, wasted anything, or done any harm?

Please forgive me.

Pastor, I have done bad things and ask you to hear my confession and to pronounce forgiveness in order to fulfill God's will.

Let it be done for you as you believe.
And I, by the command of our Lord Jesus Christ,
forgive you your sins in the name of the Father
and of the Son and of the Holy Spirit.

Amen. Go in peace.

Follow and Do

The Lord's Supper

Follow and Do
The Lord's Supper

Written and Illustrated by Joni Walker

CONCORDIA PUBLISHING HOUSE • SAINT LOUIS

Published by Concordia Publishing House
3558 S. Jefferson Avenue, St. Louis, MO 63118-3968
1-800-325-3040 · cph.org

Manufactured in China/055760/418582

9 10 11 12 13 14 15 16 17 18 35 34 33 32 31 30 29 28 27 26

For my children—
Dirk, Alivia, and Brooks
and in memory of Robert

Dear Parents,

"Come Lord Jesus. . . ." "Come, oh come, Emmanuel. . . ." "Thy kingdom come. . . ." We pray often that Christ comes to us. In the Lord's Supper, through His called and ordained servant, He does just that.

The Jesus who comes to us in **Holy Communion** is not the ethereal Jesus, the feelings-in-the-heart kind of Jesus. It is not a symbolic Christ. This Jesus places His real self in the **bread and wine**—real presence—for us. This is God in the reality of His Word and the tangible elements providing us with forgiveness, renewal, and strength.

In our **traditions**, young children do not receive the Lord's Supper, but they often have questions about it, finding it a mysterious and curious ritual.

Even little ones can learn about the special reality that Jesus still does very real things for us. Many congregations invite children to come to the altar with their parents. This allows the youngest members an up-close look at the Sacrament and teaches them the ritual long before they participate in it. In this way, parents and church alike teach children about the divine service, fulfilling an important vow made at the child's Baptism, that we "provide for his further instruction in the Christian faith, his baptismal grace and in communion with the Church."

Our Savior invites us to His table regardless of our state. We come to the altar as sinful people. We leave wrapped in His grace and filled with the PEACE that comes only from knowing His mercy and from being certain of His promises.

We don't know when Jesus will come again in the flesh or when He will call us to be with Him. Nevertheless, until then He comes to be with us in this very real way. "COME, LORD JESUS . . ." and He does!

What is the Sacrament of the Altar?

It is the true body and blood of our Lord Jesus Christ under the bread and wine, instituted by Christ Himself for us Christians to eat and to drink.

Where is this written?

The holy Evangelists Matthew, Mark, Luke, and St. Paul write:

Our Lord Jesus Christ, on the night when He was betrayed, took bread, and when He had given thanks…

He broke it and gave it to the disciples and said: "Take, eat; this is My body, which is given for you. This do in remembrance of Me."

Toni

In the same way also He took the cup after supper, and when He had given thanks,

He gave it to them, saying,

"Drink of it, all of you; this cup is the
new testament in My blood, which
is shed for you for the forgiveness of sins.
This do, as often as you drink it, in
remembrance of Me."

What is the benefit of this eating and drinking?

These words, "Given and shed for you for the forgiveness of sins," show us that in the Sacrament forgiveness of sins, life, and salvation are given us through these words. For where there is forgiveness of sins, there is also life and salvation.

How can bodily eating and drinking do such great things?

Certainly not just eating and drinking do these things, but the words written here: “Given and shed for you for the forgiveness of sins.”

Come
Spirit

These words, along with the bodily eating and drinking, are the main thing in the Sacrament. Whoever believes these words has exactly what they say: "forgiveness of sins."

Who receives this sacrament worthily?

Fasting and bodily preparation are certainly fine outward training.

But that person is truly worthy and well prepared who has faith in these words: "Given and shed for you for the forgiveness of sins."

But anyone who does not believe these words or doubts them is unworthy and unprepared, for the words **"for you"** require all hearts to believe.

Follow and Do

Holy Baptism

Follow and Do

Holy Baptism

Written and Illustrated by Joni Walker

CONCORDIA PUBLISHING HOUSE • SAINT LOUIS

Published by Concordia Publishing House
3558 S. Jefferson Avenue, St. Louis, MO 63118-3968
1-800-325-3040 · cph.org

Manufactured in China/055760/418582

9 10 11 12 13 14 15 16 17 18 35 34 33 32 31 30 29 28 27 26

For my brother Steve
and my sister Julie.

Dear Parents,

When we see our babies for the first time, it's almost impossible to comprehend the concept of ORIGINAL SIN in them. Yet it's there. Babies seem to be completely innocent; nevertheless, they are guilty of sin that separates them from a loving God.

Once and for all, Jesus overcame that separation. He went to the cross and took upon Himself the punishment for sin, original and otherwise. Now we can freely and confidently confess that we believe in one Baptism for the remission of sins and in life everlasting. As St. Paul said in Romans 6:3–5, "all of us who were baptized into Christ Jesus were baptized into His death … in order that, just as Christ was raised from the dead through the glory of the Father, we too may live a new life … united with Him in His resurrection."

From the moment we know about them, even in the months before they are born, we joyfully do all we can to care for our children so they grow physically and emotionally into healthy, happy people.

A developing child also needs other loving adults. Parents, grandparents, aunts, uncles, siblings, friends, and caregivers individually and collectively contribute to the development of our children. Among those people are the Godparents we choose, people like us who are dedicated to bringing up our child in the nurture and admonition of the Word of God.

It is our parental responsibility to bring our child forward to be baptized. God commands it. It is also our great joy because Baptism is not about what *we* do—it is about what God does. It is through the washing and renewal of water and Word that our child's sins are forgiven and faith is created, once and for all.

Beyond our own parenting efforts, our love and care are surpassed only by that given by God in His Word and Sacraments. Although we are sinners, we are saints as well, made righteous through the work of Christ. Thanks be to God!

First
What is Baptism?

Baptism is not just plain water, but it is the water included in God's command and combined with God's word.

My baby brother is going to be baptized today.

Which is that word of God?

Christ our Lord says in the last chapter of Matthew:

> "Therefore go and make disciples of all nations, baptizing them in the name of the Father and of the Son and of the Holy Spirit" (Matthew 28:19).

Would you like to come to Vacation Bible School with us?

SECOND

WHAT BENEFITS DOES BAPTISM GIVE?

It works forgiveness of sins, rescues from death and the devil,
and gives eternal salvation to all who believe this,
as the words and promises of God declare.

I am not afraid of the devil because God protects me.

Which are these words and promises of God?

Christ our Lord says in the last chapter of Mark:

> **"Whoever believes and is baptized will be saved, but whoever does not believe will be condemned" (Mark 16:16).**

I will always believe in God.

Third

How can water do such great things?

Certainly not just water, but the word of God in and with the water does these things, along with the faith which trusts this word of God in the water.

When someone is baptized
the water is special because it is
combined with God's Word.

For without God's word the water is plain water and no Baptism. But with the word of God it is a Baptism, that is, a life-giving water, rich in grace, and a washing of the new birth in the Holy Spirit, as St. Paul says in Titus, chapter three.

I am happy
that my brother
is God's child,
like me.

"He saved us through the washing of rebirth and renewal by the Holy Spirit, whom He poured out on us generously through Jesus Christ our Savior, so that, having been justified by His grace, we might become heirs having the hope of eternal life.
This is a trustworthy saying" (Titus 3:5–8).

I know that Jesus died for me.

Fourth
What does such baptizing with water indicate

It indicates that the Old Adam in us should by daily contrition and repentance be drowned and die with all sins and evil desires,

Dear God,

Forgive me for the bad things I said and did today.

and that a new man should daily emerge and arise to live before God in righteousness and purity forever.

Thank you God,
for this new day.

Where is this written?

St. Paul writes in Romans chapter six: "We were therefore buried with Him through baptism into death in order that, just as Christ was raised from the dead through the glory of the Father, we too may live a new life" (Romans 6:4).

I am glad I was baptized. Someday, I will live in heaven with Jesus.

Follow and Do

The Lord's Prayer

Follow and Do
The Lord's Prayer

Written and Illustrated by Joni Walker

CONCORDIA PUBLISHING HOUSE • SAINT LOUIS

Published by Concordia Publishing House
3558 S. Jefferson Avenue, St. Louis, MO 63118-3968
1-800-325-3040 · cph.org

Manufactured in China/055760/418582

9 10 11 12 13 14 15 16 17 18 35 34 33 32 31 30 29 28 27 26

To my husband,

Dave.

Dear Parent,

We begin with simple PRAYERS at bedtime and mealtime. Children enthusiastically learn from you to fold their hands, bow their heads, and say, "Now I Lay Me" and "Come, Lord Jesus."

At first, of course, such prayers are extensions of other verbal skill development and are on the same level as reciting the ABCs. But soon children make the connection between reciting prayers at home and praying in church, between just saying words and saying them to Someone. They begin to comprehend that praying is a holy conversation with their heavenly Father. The conversations always begin with God's Holy Word, where He teaches how to speak to Him. Therefore, when we speak in prayer, we speak the same way He speaks and we know it is good.

God invites us and expects us to pray in Jesus' name. We are free to go to Him at all times and in all places because Jesus reconciled us to God and intercedes on our behalf. Prayer is a GIFT to us as God's children and our loving Father promises to listen and answer.

Prayer helps us to keep God's will in front of us. He knows what is best for us. That is why we pray to ask Him to bring us in line with His Word and HIS WILL for us.

When Jesus' disciples asked about the proper way to pray, He gave them the model for prayer, which we call the Lord's Prayer. All forms of prayer—confession, adoration, thanksgiving, intercession—are based on this perfect model.

God calls parents to the joyous responsibility and privilege of teaching and nurturing the habit of regular, confident conversation with our heavenly Father. The confidence comes from Jesus' blood for our sins. Your child will hear the prayer Jesus taught in every worship service. When you repeat it at home, you help your child learn what Jesus gave to them, the Lord's Prayer, and connect worship life with daily life as a Christian.

"Do not be anxious about anything, but in everything, by prayer and petition, with thanksgiving, present your requests to God" (Philippians 4:6).

Our Father who art in heaven.

With these words God tenderly invites us to believe that He is our true Father and that we are His true children, so that with all boldness and confidence we may ask Him as dear children ask their dear father.

Hallowed be Thy name.

I like to learn about God.

God's name is certainly holy in itself, but we pray in this petition that it may be kept holy among us also.

Thy kingdom come.

The kingdom of God certainly comes by itself without our prayer, but we pray in this petition that it may come to us also.

Thy will be done on earth as it is in heaven.

e good and gracious will of God is done even without our prayer, t we pray in this petition that it may be done among us also.

God helps us play nicely and be kind to one another.

Give us this day our daily bread.

God certainly gives daily bread to everyone without our prayers, even to all evil people, but we pray in this petition that God would lead us to realize this and to receive our daily bread with thanksgiving.

And forgive us our trespasses as we forgive those who trespass against us.

We pray in this petition that our Father in heaven would not look at our sins, or deny our prayer because of them. We are neither worthy of the things for wh we pray, nor have we deserved them, but we ask that He would give them all to by grace, for we daily sin much and surely deserve nothing but punishment. So we too will sincerely forgive and gladly do good to those who sin against us.

I'm sorry I got
mad at you.
Let's be friends again!

And lead us not into temptation.

God tempts no one. We pray in this petition that God would guard and keep us so that the devil, the world, and our sinful nature may not deceive us or mislead us into false belief, despair, and other great shame and vice. Although we are attacked by these things, we pray that we may finally overcome them and win the victory.

Mom said we are not allowed
to have snacks
before dinner.

But deliver us from evil.

I'm glad that I will live
in heaven with God someday.

We pray in this petition, in summary,
that our Father in heaven would rescue us
from every evil of body and soul, possessions
and reputation, and finally, when our last hour
comes, give us a blessed end, and graciously take
us from this valley of sorrow to Himself in heaven.

For Thine is the kingdom and the power and the glory forever and ever.

This means that I should be certain that these petitions are pleasing to our Father in heaven, and are heard by Him; for He Himself has commanded us to pray in this way and has promised to hear us.

God likes to
hear us pray.

Amen.

"Yes, yes, it shall be so."

We know
God's word is true.

Follow and Do

God's Ten Commandments

Written and Illustrated by Joni Walker

CONCORDIA PUBLISHING HOUSE · SAINT LOUIS

Published by Concordia Publishing House
3558 S. Jefferson Avenue, St. Louis, MO 63118-3968
1-800-325-3040 · cph.org

Manufactured in China/055760/418582

9 10 11 12 13 14 15 16 17 18 35 34 33 32 31 30 29 28 27 26

Follow and Do

God's Ten Commandments

This is for Justin,

Travis,

Sarah,

Brian,

Tiff,

Heather,

Austin,

Zach,

Madison,

and Parker.

Dear Parent,

From the moment our young child begins to move about on his own, we set boundaries. Because we love him and want to keep him safe, we guide him away from harmful behaviors. As he grows, we offer additional guidelines for his interaction with other people. We say things like "please follow my directions" or "remember to say 'thank you'" with patience and consistency so our child learns. It takes time and practice, but setting boundaries and direction are outgrowths of our LOVE and care as Christian parents.

Our Father in heaven loves us and cares for us too, and He shows us this love in many ways. God provides parents, grandparents, teachers, pastors, and day care providers who take on different roles in the care and nurture of children. God provides our daily bread and His Word and Sacraments as His means of grace.

The Commandments are God's way of setting direction and boundaries for us. He uses them to show us our sin and, therefore, our need for forgiveness. He uses them to teach us how to live as His adopted children and how to live with one another as brothers and sisters in Christ. He uses them to keep us from harm. Every aspect of our everyday lives is covered by the Commandments.

Even for adults, learning to follow God's directions takes time and practice. We make mistakes or we forget and we veer away from His desires for us. Our loving Father continues to provide for us even then. God provides forgiveness through His Son, Jesus Christ, who lived the perfectly obedient life that we cannot. Through His death and resurrection, our Savior gave Himself for our sins and reconciled us to God. And because we have His gift of forgiveness, we can confidently teach, guide, direct, and love our precious child.

You shall **have no other gods.**

We should fear, love, and trust in God above all things.

You shall not
misuse the name of the Lord your God.

We should fear and love God so that we do not curse, swear, use satanic arts, lie, or deceive by His name, but call upon it in every trouble, pray, praise, and give thanks.

Remember
the Sabbath day
by keeping it holy.

We should fear and love God so that we do not despise preaching and His Word, but hold it sacred and gladly hear and learn it.

Honor
your father and your mother.

We should fear and love God so that we do not despise or anger our parents and other authorities, but honor them, serve and obey them, love and cherish them.

You shall
not murder.

We should fear and love God so that we do not hurt or harm our neighbor in his body, but help and support him in every physical need.

You shall
not commit adultery.

We should fear and love God so that we lead a sexually pure and decent life in what we say and do, and husband and wife love and honor each other.

God wants Mom and Dad to love only each other.

You shall
not steal.

We should fear and love God so that we do not take our neighbor's money or possessions, or get them in any dishonest way, but help him to improve and protect his possessions and income.

We should fear and love God so that we do not tell lies about our neighbor, betray him, slander him, or hurt his reputation, but defend him, speak well of him, and explain everything in the kindest way.

You shall not give false testimony against your neighbor

I did not treat him very nicely and I want to tell him that I am sorry.

You shall not covet your neighbor's house.

We should fear and love God so that we do not scheme to get our neighbor's inheritance or house, or get it in a way which only appears right, but help and be of service to him in keeping it.

8160

You shall not

covet your neighbor's wife or manservant or maidservant, his ox or donkey, or anything that belongs to your neighbor.

We should fear and love God
so that we do not entice or force
away our neighbor's wife, workers,
or animals, or turn them against him,
but urge them to stay and do their duty.

Follow and Do

The Apostles' Creed

Written and Illustrated by Joni Walker

CONCORDIA PUBLISHING HOUSE • SAINT LOUIS

Published by Concordia Publishing House
3558 S. Jefferson Avenue, St. Louis, MO 63118-3968
1-800-325-3040 · cph.org

Manufactured in China/055760/418582

9 10 11 12 13 14 15 16 17 18 35 34 33 32 31 30 29 28 27 26

For my dear friends—

Bud and Esther,
Don and Helen,
Emery,
Ceil,
Hazel,
and Joan.

Also in memory of Carl.

Dear Parents,

Webster's defines "creed" as "a brief authoritative formula of religious belief; a set of fundamental beliefs; a guiding principle." We confess the Apostles' Creed, as well as the two other creeds of the Christian church, as a statement of our faith in the Triune God. The Apostles' Creed is also known as the baptismal creed. It is confessed by the church at Baptism because we are baptized at Christ's command in the name of the Triune God.

The Creed is a concise, emphatic summary of what Scripture teaches about God the Father, Son, and Holy Spirit. Since the second or third century, Christians across the ages and around the world have spoken these words to express what we believe God does in our world and in our lives.

After they teach their children the Lord's Prayer, many parents teach the Apostles' Creed so their young ones can continue to learn about worshiping God and learn how to receive God's gifts in the church service. Regardless when parents choose to teach about the faith, when they do, they are fulfilling their calling as Christian parents. "Let the word of Christ dwell in you richly as you teach and admonish one another with all wisdom, and as you SING psalms, hymns and spiritual songs with gratitude in your hearts to God" (Colossians 3:16).

Young children learn through all their senses. They remember experiences and they like repetition. Because they delight in memorizing, children readily learn to say the Creed and absorb the meaning of its three articles: that God the Father created us, God the Son redeemed us, and God the Holy Spirit sanctifies us.

The tone and cadence of the Creed spoken in church becomes a lasting MEMORY that is combined with other sensory dynamics, such as music, sights, smells, and the like. And when our children hear us say these words in church week after week, they begin to understand and appreciate our faith in God as well. As they do, they see themselves—and us—as God's baptized, forgiven, and redeemed children.

The First Article–Creation

**I believe in God, the Father Almighty,
Maker of heaven and earth.**

God created the world.

WHAT DOES THIS MEAN?

I believe that God has made me and all creatures; that He has given me my body and soul, eyes, ears, and all my members, my reason and all my senses, and still takes care of them.

God made each of us special.

He also gives me clothing and shoes, food and drink, house and home, wife and children, land, animals, and all I have. He richly and daily provides me with all that I need to support this body and life.

I am thankful for
the family
God gave me.

He defends me against all danger and guards and protects me from all evil. All this He does only out of fatherly, divine goodness and mercy, without any merit or worthiness in me. For all this it is my duty to thank and praise, serve and obey Him.
This is most certainly true.

Thank You God, for protecting me.

The Second Article–Redemption

And in Jesus Christ, His only Son, our Lord, who was conceived by the Holy Spirit, born of the Virgin Mary, suffered under Pontius Pilate, was crucified, died and was buried. He descended into hell. The third day He rose again from the dead. He ascended into heaven and sits at the right hand of God, the Father Almighty. From thence He will come to judge the living and the dead

I am glad Jesus died to take my sins away.

WHAT DOES THIS MEAN?

I believe that Jesus Christ true God, begotten of the Father from eternity, and also true man, born of the Virgin Mary, is my Lord, who has redeemed me, a lost and condemned person, purchased and won me from all sins, from death, and from the power of the devil; not with gold or silver, but with His holy, precious blood and with His innocent suffering and death, that I may be His own and live under Him in His kingdom and serve Him in everlasting righteousness, innocence, and blessedness, just as He is risen from the dead, lives and reigns to all eternity. This is most certainly true.

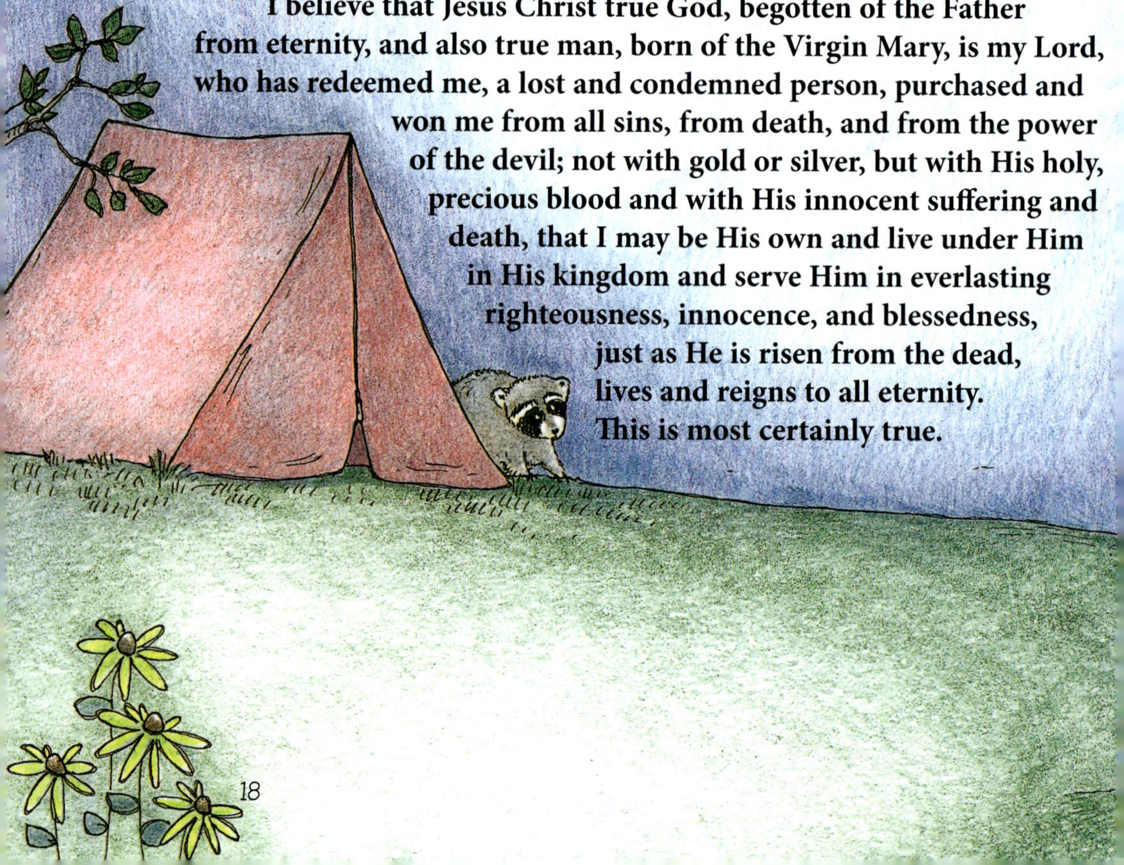

Jesus loves me . . .

The Third Article–Sanctification

I believe in the Holy Spirit, the holy Christian church, the communion of saints, the forgiveness of sins, the resurrection of the body, and the life everlasting. Amen.

I love to be with my family in church.

WHAT DOES THIS MEAN?

I believe that I cannot by my own reason or strength believe in Jesus Christ, my Lord, or come to Him; but the Holy Spirit has called me by the Gospel, enlightened me with His gifts, sanctified and kept me in the true faith.

When I read the Bible, the Holy Spirit is keeping me in my faith.

In the same way He calls, gathers, enlightens, and sanctifies the whole Christian church on earth, and keeps it with Jesus Christ in the one true faith. In this Christian church He daily and richly forgives all my sins and the sins of all believers.

God is happy when
we come to hear Him.

On the Last Day He will raise me and all the dead, and give eternal life to me and all believers in Christ. This is most certainly true.

I will see great-grandpa
and grandma in heaven someday.

Follow and Do

The Apostles' Creed